The Sea Power Library

FRIGATES

The Sea Power Library

FRIGATES

by Max Walmer

Rourke Publications, Inc.
Vero Beach, Florida 32964

John L. Hall, *a Perry-class frigate, at speed.*

Library of Congress Cataloging-in-Publication Data

Walmer, Max.
   Frigates.
   (The Sea power library)
   Includes index.
   Summary: Describes the history, types, weapons, and present uses of frigates, both in the United States and the Soviet Union.
    1. Frigates — Juvenile literature. [1. Frigates]
I. Title. II. Series.
V826.W35   1989   359.3'2   88-30695
ISBN 0-86625-0820-4

Contents

Duties

The name "frigate" for a class of warship is an old one. It was originally given by the French in the eighteenth century to describe a sailing ship that was slightly smaller, less heavily armed, but faster than the contemporary **line-of-battle ships**. Such ships acted as scouts for the main battle fleet but did not

There are 96 frigates in the active fleet of the U.S. Navy and more than half of these are of the Oliver Hazard Perry class.

Almost half the frigate fleet consists of Knox-class ships, each of which has a displacement of 4,200 tons fully loaded.

themselves normally join the line of battle in a major engagement. Unlike line-of-battle ships, which carried their cannon on two, three or four decks, frigates carried all their armament on one deck. The number of cannons ranged from twenty-four to fifty. The name "frigate" is thus older in origin than those of other types of modern warships, such as "destroyer" and "cruiser."

During the 25 years of conflict in Europe that followed the French Revolution of 1789, all the navies involved used frigates to obtain information about the operations of enemy fleets. Admirals were always desperate for information about enemy ships, and the British Admiral Horatio Nelson voiced the views of all when he complained regularly and bitterly that he never had enough frigates. Although not involved in the Napoleonic Wars, the U.S. Navy built some very successful frigates. The three largest — *United States, Constitution,* and *President* — were built in the late 1790s. They mounted thirty 24-pound "long guns" and twenty-two 42-pound "carronades" and scored some notable successes over ships of the British Royal Navy when war broke out between the two countries in 1812.

A Perry-class frigate, such as the USS Crommelin, *is powered by two General Electric gas-turbine engines that deliver a top speed of almost 30 knots.*

On August 19, 1812, Captain Isaac Hull in the **USS** *Constitution* totally demolished the British frigate **HMS** *Guerriere* in just thirty minutes off the Nova Scotia coast. Two months later the USS *United States* under command of Captain Stephen Decatur took 90 minutes to dismast and overpower HMS *Macedonian* off the Portuguese island of Madeira. The British ship was then brought back to Newport, Rhode Island, refitted, and pressed into service against her former owners. In December the USS *Constitution,* now under the command of Captain William Bainbridge (an officer nicknamed "Old Ironsides") met and defeated HMS *Java* near the port of Bahia in Brazil.

Perry-class frigates carry over 200 officers and enlisted men. ▶

◀ *Several Perry-class frigates have been modified to accommodate LAMPS helicopters.*

The principal gun on the Perry class is a 76mm Melara, capable of firing 90 rounds per minute. ▼

Not all U.S. frigates were so successful, however. The USS *Chesapeake,* despite the exceptional bravery of her captain and crew, was defeated by HMS *Shannon* in a famous engagement off Boston, Massachusetts on June 1, 1813.

Of these illustrious United States frigates, one is not only still in existence, but actually remains in commission as a ship of the U.S. Navy. That one is the USS *Constitution,* which first went to sea on July 22,

Tied up at a pier, the frigate **Rodney M. Davis** *shows its starboard bow just after construction is completed.*

1798. She is docked at the former Boston Navy Yard and is taken out into the bay once a year and turned to prevent her old timbers from warping.

Starboard beam view of the Rodney M. Davis *under way during sea trials off the coast of southern California.*

USS Knox, *the flagship of its class, shows off its forward 5-inch gun.*

A starbold amidships view of the bridge and superstructure of the *Rodney M. Davis.*

The aft section of the Perry-class frigates has provision for storage and operation of two LAMPS helicopters.

A view of the main engine room aboard the **Rodney M. Davis.**

The name "frigate" continued to be applied to such sailing warships until about 1850, when the name disappeared. All ships so named at that time were redesignated "cruisers." The name next appeared in the middle of World War Two. The majority of British anti-submarine warfare (**ASW**) ships at the start of the war were "corvettes," small ships of some 800 tons **displacement,** based upon the design of large, ocean-going trawlers. These ships proved to be very successful, although they were not quite large enough for all the weapons systems and sensors that were coming into use in the battle against German U-boats. These corvettes were a little slow, and they were particularly uncomfortable for their crews in the wild waters of the North Atlantic. The British therefore decided to build larger, 1,400-ton ships for the ASW mission. In 1943 they announced that these ships would be designated frigates.

Since then, the British and other European navies have used the name "frigate" to describe warships of between 2,000 and 4,000 tons displacement, usually with a primary ASW mission. Destroyers, on the other hand, are generally of 5,000 to 9,000 tons displacement, usually with a primary anti-aircraft warfare (**AAW**) mission. Smaller than a destroyer, the frigate is in some ways a utility destroyer, designed to provide ASW protection for **task groups** and convoys, but also mounting some anti-surface and anti-aircraft weapons systems and sensors.

13

In the middle of World War Two the U.S. Navy also produced new classes of small ASW ships, similar to the British frigate. These were designated "destroyer escorts" (**DE**). The DEs of the famous Edsall class, for example, displaced 1,850 tons and were armed with three 3-inch guns, eight 40mm anti-aircraft guns, three torpedo tubes, and Hedgehog ASW depth bomb throwers. Powered by diesel engines, they had a speed of 21 **knots,** which was sufficient for the convoy and submarine speeds of those days. More destroyer escorts were built in the early 1950s to counter the growing threat from the submarines of the Soviet Navy.

The air-conditioning machinery room shows the confined space in which engineers and technicians must operate.

From here, crew members monitor all communications between the ship and shore installations.

The name "frigate" was then re-introduced into the U.S. Navy for the first time since the 1850s. This time it was used to describe much larger warships than those called frigates in the European navies. These American ships displaced around 6,000 tons and were designed to act as **flagships** for groups of destroyers accompanying a heavy task group. These were later redesignated "destroyer leaders." Some large, nuclear-powered warships with a similar task of escorting task groups were also built in the 1960s as "frigates," but these have since been redesignated "cruisers." In fact, the American use of the designation "frigate" for these larger and more capable ships was more appropriate than the British use of the same term for small ASW ships. By the mid-1960s, however, the term "frigate" was in such widespread use among other **NATO** navies that the U.S. Navy found it best to fall into line. In the late 1960s, the U.S. Navy started to build a new type of ASW ship, larger in size than the previous destroyer escorts and with a displacement of 3,000 tons. These American ships were so similar in size and role to the European frigates that they too were given the designation "frigate."

The U.S. Navy has conducted a consistent program of frigate development, which started with the Bronstein class of the 1960s. All are of 3,000 to 4,000 tons displacement, with at least one 5-inch gun, a mix of ASW weapons, an **ASROC** launcher (except for the latest Oliver Hazard Perry class), four or six tubes for ASW torpedoes, and an ASW helicopter. All have a single propeller and crews of 200 to 250 officers and ratings. The U.S. Navy now has 116 frigates in service of six classes: Bronstein — two; Glover — one; Garcia — ten; Brooke — six; Knox — forty-one; and Oliver Hazard Perry — fifty-one. Of these, twenty-four are in the Naval Reserve Force, but all the others are in front-line service. This is by far the largest frigate force in any navy.

In this section, technicians monitor radar systems which identify aircraft observed by the ship's radar.

Perry Class

Three Perry-class boats at speed.

In the 1960s the U.S. Navy planned to build two classes of anti-submarine/anti-aircraft warfare (ASW/AAW) ships in what was termed at the time a "high/low mix." The "high value" class was to be a large, sophisticated and costly destroyer, such as the Spruance and Arleigh Burke classes, whose primary mission was to protect aircraft carriers.

Not even the resources of the U.S. Navy, however, could afford such expensive ships in the large numbers needed for the escort mission. Thus the "high-value" class was to be balanced by a "low-value" warship, which was to be a class described as "patrol frigates." The very successful class of patrol frigates which resulted is named the Oliver Hazard Perry class, after the first ship to be completed. In the design stage, strict limits were placed on the maximum size of the ships, on the crew numbers, and on the total cost. The design and cost criteria were met, and ships in this class were purchased in large numbers. When the last ship, the USS *Ingraham* was completed in December 1988, fifty-one had been built, making this the largest single class of major warship to be built since World War Two.

Perry-class frigates carry a large range of radar and identification equipment.

To enable them to be built in smaller shipyards, construction techniques were kept simple. The maximum use was made of flat panels and bulkheads, and care was taken to ensure that passageways were kept straight. Also, the hull structures were prefabricated in modules of 35, 100, 200, or 400 tons each, and the shipyards were allowed to select the size most convenient to their construction needs.

Like all U.S. Navy frigates, the *Oliver Hazard Perry* has only one shaft and one propeller. The engine-room layout is much more compact than in earlier classes due to the use of gas-turbine propulsion. Two General Electric LM2500 gas turbines (the same model as used in the larger Spruance- and Arleigh Burke-class destroyers) are located side-by-side in a single engine room. In an unusual arrangement, the gas turbines are supplemented by two retractable "propulsion pods," mounted well forward, which are primarily intended to assist in docking. These pods also can be used to provide emergency "get-home" power, if needed. Each pod has a 325 horsepower engine and both working together can propel the ship at 6 knots.

USS Nicholas *shows the clean lines of its starboard bow during a high-speed turn.*

From left to right, Perry-class destroyers Hawes, Simpson *and* Elrod.

Perry-class frigates carry radar for long-range search, search and navigation, and weapons control.

USS **Flatley** *heals to port in a choppy sea.*

The Oliver Hazard Perry class is capable of anti-air, anti-surface and anti-submarine operations. Immediately forward of the bridge is a Mark 13 single-arm launcher, which can fire either Standard surface-to-air missiles or Harpoon anti-ship missiles. The missile magazine under the launcher carries four Harpoon and thirty-two Standard missiles. A gun is mounted, although its turret is such a small and neat design that it can be overlooked when examining photographs. The gun is a 3-inch weapon, located on the upper deck just in front of the stack. The gun and turret are designed by Oto Melara in Italy, and their use in a U.S. warship class is a good example of the interchange of weapons systems between partners in the NATO Alliance. The gun can be used against aircraft, ships, or ground targets ashore; it is fully automatic, with a firing rate of 85 rounds per minute and a maximum range against surface targets of 11.93 miles. Main ASW weapons systems are two **LAMPS** helicopters and two torpedo tubes firing Mark 46 ASW torpedoes.

The early ships of the class operate two LAMPS-I helicopters. This helicopter is the Kaman SH-2F Seasprite, a three-place, twin-engined machine, which carries three types of sensor: radar, **sonobuoys** and **MAD.** The radar, mounted under the nose of the SH-2F, is used to detect objects such as a ship or the periscope of a submarine running near the surface. Sonobuoys are small cylindrical devices used to detect submerged submarines by the noise they emit. The sonobuoy is dropped from the helicopter by parachute and then floats on the surface for several hours transmitting signals to the helicopter by radio. Its final function is to self-destruct by sinking to the bottom to avoid being captured and copied by potential enemies. The other ASW sensor is the Magnetic Anomaly Detector (MAD). A submarine is a large metallic body and when moving through the water it cuts through the Earth's lines of magnetic force. The MAD detector makes use of this phenomenon and is mounted in a "bird," which is towed on a cable behind the helicopter. The men in the helicopter crew also act as sensors, using what is known colloquially as the "Mark One Eyeball" (visual observation). When any of these sensor systems spots a hostile submarine, the SH-2F can attack it using its armament of two Mark 46 lightweight homing ASW torpedoes.

USS **Sprague** *carries the U.S. flag to foreign countries.*

Each Perry-class frigate has two triple torpedo tubes.

Perry-class frigates carry a crew of approximately 106.

USS **Ford** *picks up speed on a calm sea.*

Twenty-six ships of the Oliver Hazard Perry class are fitted to operate two of the more sophisticated Sikorsky SH-60B Seahawk LAMPS-II helicopters. Because the SH-60B is larger, the afterdeck area has been extended on these ships about 6 feet by increasing the rake of the stern. In addition, the Recovery Assistance, Securing, and Traversing System (**RAST**) is fitted, which enables the helicopters to take off and land even when the flight-deck is pitching and tossing in rough weather. The SH-60B, being larger and more powerful than the SH-2F, carries more powerful sensors, is faster and has a greater range, but the operating principles are the same as those just described for the smaller LAMPS-I.

Frigates of this class are constantly on patrol on the world's oceans, supporting the United States' interests and assisting allies. For example, USS *Stark* was acting in such a role, protecting tankers in the Persian Gulf, when she was hit by an Iraqi Exocet missile, on May 17, 1987. In that attack 37 sailors of the U.S. Navy were killed, defending the principle that ships of all nations should be free to navigate safely in international waters.

The Oliver Hazard Perry-class ships displace 3,605 tons at full load. They have a maximum speed of 29 knots and a range of 4,200 nautical miles at a speed of 20 knots. Besides the fifty-one ships built for the U.S. Navy, four have been built for and sold to the Royal Australian Navy. The Bazan Yard at Ferrol in Spain is building five for the Royal Spanish Navy. The Oliver Hazard Perry class is thus by far the largest single frigate class in the world.

Perry-class frigates are capable of a top speed of almost 30 knots and have a range of 4,500 miles at 20 knots.

Soviet Frigates

The second largest navy in the world is that of the Soviet Union. Their fleet has grown from a coastal force in the 1950s to the point where today they have a capability in every one of the world's oceans. The Soviet navy is not yet as powerful as the U.S. Navy. It currently lacks any major aircraft carriers and is thus unable to project air power in any significant way at sea. Nevertheless, with every year that passes, the Soviet navy is becoming more powerful and efficient. Already it has some air-capable ships of the Kiev class at sea. Also, the first of its large Kremlin-class nuclear-powered aircraft carriers is now fitting out and will join the Soviet fleet in the early 1990s.

In this expansion program Soviet naval designers have produced some excellent designs. Among the best is that of the Krivak-class frigates, which are direct equivalents to the Oliver Hazard Perry class. It is fascinating to compare these two ships.

There are now three versions of the Soviet ships in service, designated Krivak-I, Krivak-II, and Krivak-III. The first of these, Krivak-I, was initially detected by Western observers in 1970. Its long, sleek lines, ingenious combination of armament, and effective propulsion system have given rise to much admiring comment. Like the U.S. Navy's Oliver Hazard Perry class, the Krivaks are designed for ease of construction. This enables them to be built in some of the smaller naval yards in the Baltic and Black Seas, freeing the larger yards to build bigger and more complicated warships, such as destroyers and cruisers.

Soviet naval forces operate Krivak-I frigates, equipped for anti-submarine and anti-aircraft warfare.

Soviet frigates frequently operate in cooperation with guided-missile cruisers such as this Slava-class boat.

At the Nikolayev yard on the Black Sea, Soviet ships stock up with supplies for Cuba and Nicaragua.

Expanding Soviet naval interests include the use of large vessels like the Frunze *guided-missile cruiser.*

Expanding Soviet naval interests include the use of large vessels like the Frunze *guided-missile cruiser.*

Twenty-one Krivak-Is were built between 1970 and 1982. The primary mission of these ships is anti-submarine, and the most important weapons system is the **SS-N-**14, which is mounted in a large quadruple launcher on the foredeck. SS-N-14 is a missile propelled by a solid-fuel rocket motor and is launched from a tube. The missile carries an ASW homing torpedo, which it releases near the target. The torpedo then descends under a parachute to the sea, where its motor is activated and it starts a circular search pattern until its sensors detect the target submarine. Its maximum range is around 30 nautical miles, and its minimum range is 4. The Krivak-I has no underdeck magazine full of reload missiles, as do the ships of the Oliver Hazard Perry class. On the Krivaks there are just four launch tubes with four missiles — that is it.

Soviet ships are designed to refuel at sea and continue to operate in foreign waters without returning to base.

28

The Krivaks have eight 21-inch torpedo tubes, firing ASW torpedoes. In addition, for the ASW mission, two **RBU**-6000 ASW depth charge launchers are carried just forward of the bridge. Each launcher consists of twelve short barrels, arranged in a horseshoe, and fired in paired sequence. The depth charges are rocket-propelled, with a maximum range

Soviet naval forces include ships capable of moving light missile-patrol boats to wherever they are needed.

of 6,562 yards. The launcher is reloaded automatically from a below-deck magazine. This system, which has no real Western equivalent, is widely used on Soviet warships. Different models have various combinations of barrels and ranges.

Anti-surface armament is composed of four 76mm automatic guns, mounted in two twin turrets. Because missile launchers occupy the foredeck, the guns are mounted aft. This positioning could cause complications in a surface action, where the captain would have to turn away from a target ahead of his ship to enable the guns to bear on the target and fire.

A reconnaissance picture of the harbor at Al Bluff, Nicaragua, where Soviet ships are unloading weapons.

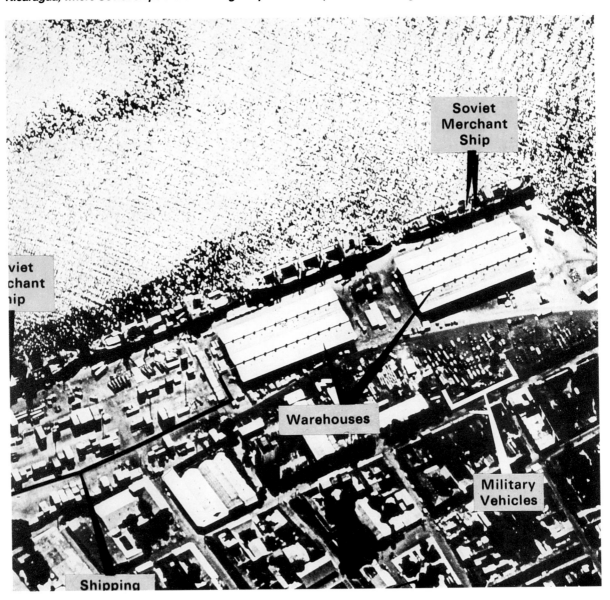

Soviet Merchant Ship

Soviet Merchant Ship

Warehouses

Military Vehicles

Shipping

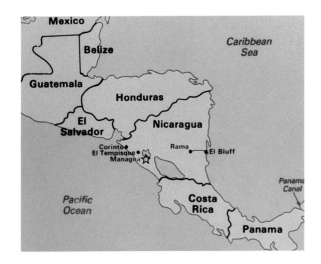

Ports on the Caribbean and Pacific Ocean shores of Nicaragua are frequently used to offload Soviet munitions.

Kirov-class battle cruisers help to extend the presence of Soviet naval power on the world's oceans.

Because the U.S.S.R. is a northern land mass, only the Pacific coastline provides ready access to the world's oceans, and Soviet naval forces are concentrated very heavily in this region.

FAR EAST TVD

DIVISIONS	53
TANKS	14,900
ARTILLERY/MORTAR	15,200
TACTICAL AIRCRAFT	1,690

PACIFIC FLEET

AIRCRAFT CARRIERS	2
PRINCIPAL SURFACE COMBATANTS	85
OTHER COMBATANT SHIPS/CRAFT	354
AUXILIARIES	235*
SUBMARINES	110*
NAVAL AVIATION	500
NAVAL INFANTRY DIVISION	1

PACIFIC TVD

* NOT INCLUDING SSBNs

Sovremenny-class destroyers each carry a helicopter used to spot targets over the horizon for their guided missiles.

Anti-aircraft armament consists of two twin **SA-N-**4 missile launchers, one on the foredeck behind the SS-N-14 launcher and the second immediately behind the stack. The SA-N-4 launchers are normally hidden below deck, the only evidence of their existence being the round hatch covers on the deck.

In 1975 a slightly different version of the Krivak appeared, designated Krivak-II. The changes included the substitution of two single 100mm guns for the two twin 76mms and some other more minor differences. Eleven Krivak-IIs have been built.

Western commentators had always said that the principal deficiency in the Krivak design was that they could not carry ASW helicopters as the U.S. Navy's Oliver Hazard Perry frigates do. In 1984 the first of the Krivak-III class was seen. One of the major changes was the fitting of a large helicopter deck aft, with a hangar to the rear of the stack. This, of course, replaced the gun turrets and one of the SA-N-4 missile launchers. A single 100mm gun turret is mounted on the foredeck, displacing the SS-N-14 ASW missile launcher. In addition, two 30mm gatling **CIWS** turrets have been added, one either side of the helicopter hangar, for close-in protection.

The Krivak-III, however, is not classified by the Soviets as a *Storozhevoy Korabl'* (patrol ship), as are the Krivak-I and Krivak-II. Instead, it is classified as *Pogranichnyy Storozhevoy Korabl'*, which means border patrol ship. These frigates have been designed for and are operated by the Maritime Border Guard Service of the Soviet Secret Police — the KGB. In fact, they are even named after two heroes of the KGB, *Menzhinskiy* and *Dzerzhinskiy*. Their stated mission is to patrol the Soviet Union's sea borders, although they seem exceptionally well-armed for such a task. The helicopter, a Kamov Ka-27 Helix, is not an ASW version of this Soviet Navy helicopter. It appears to be carried in order to expand the ship's patrol area.

Like the Oliver Hazard Perry class, the Krivaks are powered by gas turbines, although the concept is somewhat different. The Soviet ships have two propellers, with two gas turbines on each shaft: a cruise turbine of 12,000 horsepower and a 24,300 horsepower boost turbine for maximum speed. These give the Krivaks a flank speed of 32 knots and a range of 3,900 nautical miles at 20 knots, compared to the Oliver Hazard Perry's 30 knots and 4,200 nautical miles at 20 knots.

*This dramatic shot of the **Frunze** guided-missile battle cruiser displays the modern design characteristics of Soviet naval vessels.*

The Oliver Hazard Perry frigates have just a few antennas on the mast and superstructure, whereas the Krivaks have more visible antennas, and they are much larger. It might seem, therefore, that the Soviet ships are better equipped. In fact, the opposite is true. American electronic technology is more advanced than that in the Soviet Union, and the more sophisticated and capable U.S. radar sets need fewer antennas.

In all, twenty-one Krivak-Is and eleven Krivak-IIs serve in the four major Soviet Navy fleets: Northern (based in Murmansk), Baltic, Black Sea, and Pacific. They are seen by Western observers in all the oceans of the world, either acting as ASW escorts for larger warships, such as Kiev-class aircraft carriers, or on independent missions. Both KGB Krivak-IIIs are deployed in the Pacific.

The largest Soviet naval base outside the U.S.S.R. is at Cam Ranh Bay in Vietnam.

Operations

Frigates are one of the most useful types of modern warships. They are capable of acting in escort groups to provide ASW protection for task groups of major warships, such as aircraft carriers or battleships, or for merchant ship convoys. Most frigates are also sufficiently well-armed and equipped to be able to act individually, when the need arises, although not in a high threat environment. As happens so often with modern defense equipment, frigates have grown in size and complexity over the years. The British frigates of 1943 displaced about 1,300 tons, while today's frigates have an average displacement of about 4,000 tons, making them over three times as large.

A typical convoy escort group might include between five and ten frigates, together with two or three destroyers to provide air defense. All the ships of the escort group would be linked by radio communications, providing both voice and data communications. The latter enable the sensors and

Ships in an escort group must operate closely and effectively together, relying heavily on ship-to-ship communications to coordinate escort and attack plans.

computers in the various ships to link up with each other, to exchange information, and to update each other. At least one-third of the available ASW helicopters would be airborne on ASW patrol at all times, operating outside the range of the ASW sensors on board the ships themselves. In addition, it is likely that such a group would have a nuclear-powered, hunter-killer submarine working in the area. Cooperating with the surface ships, the submarine would look in particular for hostile submarines lurking deep below the surface, lying in wait for the convoy and its escorts.

Finally, the convoy might also include some land- or carrier-based ASW aircraft that would give further support to the escort group.

Frigates are one of the most useful types of warship because they can be used in diverse roles such as anti-submarine warfare or escort ships for large warships.

SS *Mayaguez*

One of the more unusual real-life adventures to befall a U.S. frigate occurred in 1975, shortly after the final withdrawal from Vietnam. On May 12 the frigate USS *Harold E. Holt* was under way in the South China Sea when her captain received a signal that a U.S. merchant ship, SS *Mayaguez,* on lawful passage in international waters in the Gulf of Thailand, had been seized by gunboats belonging to the Khmer Rouge regime in Cambodia (now known as Kampuchea). President Ford ordered immediate, firm action to counter this act of high seas piracy.

Frigates like the USS **Samuel B. Roberts** *must remain constantly on alert and ready to defend U.S. or friendly foreign forces at any time.*

USS Cook, *a Knox-class guided-missile frigate.*

International incidents can sometimes be checked and kept at a low level by prompt action on the part of U.S. naval forces.

As frequently happens in the early stages of an unexpected international incident, the situation was confused, and very little information was available to U.S. rescuers. The radio operator of the *Mayaguez* sent a brief signal as the crew was overpowered by the Khmer Rouge. His signal was intercepted by an American radio operator in far-off Jakarta, Indonesia; he, in turn, passed the message on to Washington, D.C., via the U.S. Embassy. Other than that, all that was known for sure was that *Mayaguez* was anchored off a small island called Koh Tang. Far more important than the ship was the safety of the crew, and there was no information at all as to their whereabouts. Lacking any information to the contrary, U.S. officials assumed that they must be on the island.

Control and coordination of the response to an unprovoked threat frequently involves ships of many types, and sometimes both naval and marine forces.

A group of 223 U.S. marines was flown from Okinawa to an airbase in Thailand and from there they were ferried by U.S. Air Force HH-53 and CH-53 helicopters to Koh Tang. As the first wave of helicopters came in to land on the beaches of the island, they were greeted by a hail of fire from

The values of making friendly visits to foreign ports is enhanced when information is obtained that may be useful in time of war.

automatic weapons. With great courage, the pilots managed to get their men ashore. One helicopter, code number K21, incurred about 75 hits, including at least one from a rocket. In the first hour of the action no less than three helicopters were shot down; the others were seriously damaged although still flyable.

Carried on the stern of all Perry-class frigates, helicopters are vital for the ships' wartime effectiveness.

USS *Holt,* meanwhile, had reached the *Mayaguez.* A naval boarding party repossessed her, only to find her totally deserted. Meanwhile, another U.S. warship, the destroyer USS *Henry B. Wilson,* was also heading at high speed for Koh Tang. As she passed near the Cambodian coast, her captain was surprised to see a small local fishing boat flying a white flag approaching his ship. Naturally, the boat was treated with some suspicion, but it turned out to have the missing *Mayaguez* crewmen on board. They had been taken to the mainland port of Sihanoukville, rather than to Koh Tang, and *Mayaguez'* skipper, Captain Charles T. Miller, had persuaded the Khmer Rouge to release them, a decision no doubt helped by the very determined action then taking place against Koh Tang. Fortunately, the crew members were safe and well, if somewhat dazed by their experience. As the fishing boat returned home the crew returned to the *Mayaguez,* which was soon under way and out of the area.

USS Doyle *shows her forward 76mm gun.*

Perry-class frigates carry Harpoon and Standard
surface-to-surface and surface-to-air missiles.

Maneuverability is important for a fast-moving ship
responding to surprise attack.

The task group next turned to the problem of recovering the marines from the island, where they were still embroiled in a violent battle with the Khmer Rouge forces. Fortunately, the aircraft carrier USS *Coral Sea* was now only about 70 miles away. Not only were her attack aircraft able to give fire support to the embattled marines, but the air force helicopters already involved in the battle were able to use her flight deck for refueling and hasty repairs.

USS *Holt* and *Wilson* were now off the island and

The USS Samuel B. Roberts *makes a gentle turn to starboard in a calm sea.*

both became heavily involved. A longboat crewed by sailors from the *Wilson* and armed with two heavy machine-guns went close enough to shore to give covering fire to the marines ashore, while *Wilson's* own 5-inch main gun destroyed a beached Cambodian gunboat that was being used by a small party of Cambodian snipers.

As darkness fell it was decided to complete the evacuation of the marines, whose presence on the island was no longer necessary. Three helicopters went in and picked up parties of marines; two went off to unload on the *Coral Sea,* about 20 minutes' flying time away, but Lieutenant Blough, captain of helicopter code number JG44, decided to save time by using the USS *Holt,* which was just off the shore. To offload men from such a large helicopter onto a frigate's tiny flight-deck in daylight would have been considered extremely dangerous, but Lieutenant Blough did it at night in a helicopter riddled with bullet holes and with his landing lights shot out! He approached the frigate with his flight-crewman hanging out of the helicopter's door giving directions. A landing of sorts was made, but only one mainwheel could touch the flight-deck and there was just 2 feet clearance between the whirling rotor blade and the hangar corner-post! As soon as the marines were safely offloaded, the helicopter headed back to the island and picked up another load. On this trip power-loss was experienced on one of the damaged engines, and Lieutenant Blough felt that a repeat landing on the USS *Holt* would be unwise. He went off to the USS *Coral Sea* instead.

American sailors, marines, and airmen showed great courage and determination throughout this day-long action. Fifteen Americans were killed and many more wounded, but the mission — the early release of the crew of SS *Mayaguez* — was achieved. The crews of the two navy warships found themselves, like their air force and marine colleagues, thrust quite unexpectedly into a combat situation. Whether they were boarding the *Mayaguez,* shelling the island, taking armed longboats close inshore, or providing landing platforms for large helicopters, they performed their tasks magnificently.

USS **Vreeland,** *a Knox-class guided-missile frigate.*

Abbreviations

AAW	Anti-Aircraft Warfare
ASROC	Anti-Submarine Rocket
ASW	Anti-Submarine Warfare
CIWS	Close-In Weapons System
	A multi-barreled gun with a very high rate of fire for "last-ditch" protection, especially against missiles.
DE	Destroyer Escorts
HMS	Her Majesty's Ship
	Designation for warships of the British Royal Navy, such as HMS *Invincible*.
LAMPS	Light Airborne Multi-Purpose System
	U.S. Navy helicopter-borne ASW system. The two LAMPS helicopters in service are LAMPS-I, the Kamen SH-2F Seasprite, and LAMPS-II, The Sikorsky SH-60B Seahawk.
MAD	Magnetic Anomaly Detector
	A device for detecting submerged submarines.
NATO	North Atlantic Treaty Organization
RAST	Recovery Assistance, Securing, and Traversing System
SAM	Surface-to-Air Missile
SA-N-	Surface-to-Air — Navy
	U.S. Navy designator for Soviet SAM systems deployed on board warships. Always followed by a type number such as SA-N-4.
SSM	Surface-to-Surface Missile
SS-N-	Surface-to-Surface — Navy
	U.S. Navy designator for Soviet SSM systems deployed on boats and warships. Always followed by a type number, such as SS-N-2.
USS	United States Ship
	Designation for a warship of the United States Navy, such as USS *Bronstein*.

Glossary

Displacement

The measure of the size of a ship, given by the amount of water it displaces. Figures given in this book are for "full-load displacement," when the ship is fully armed, equipped, and loaded for war.

Flagship

The ship in a task group that holds the commanding admiral's headquarters. It flies his flag to indicate this role.

Knot

The measure of speed at sea.
1 knot = 1 nautical mile per hour.

Line-of-battle ships

Major warships in the sailing era, which took their place "in the line" when engaging the enemy fleet, which would also be in line. Frigates were considered too lightly armed to take their place in the line. The term was eventually shortened to "battleships," meaning the heaviest, gun-armed warships.

Nautical mile

1 nautical mile = 1.1515 statute miles
             = 6,082 feet

Sonobuoys

Small cylindrical devices used to detect submerged submarines by the noise they emit.

Task group

A tactical grouping of warships, assembled to carry out a particular task.

Index

Page references in *italics* indicate photographs or illustrations.